Bond

STRETCH
Non-verbal Reasoning
Tests and Papers

10–11+ years

Alison Primrose

Nelson Thornes

Published in 2012 by:
Nelson Thornes Ltd
Delta Place
27 Bath Road
CHELTENHAM
GL53 7TH
United Kingdom

12 13 14 15 16 / 10 9 8 7 6 5 4 3 2 1

A catalogue record for this book is available from the British Library

ISBN 978 1 4085 1867 0

Illustrations by Peters & Zabransky
Page make-up by eMC Design Ltd
Printed and bound in Spain by GraphyCems

Introduction

What is Bond?

The Bond Stretch series is a new addition to the Bond range of Assessment papers, the number one series for the 11+, selective exams and general practice. Bond Stretch is carefully designed to challenge above and beyond the level provided in the regular Bond assessment range.

How does this book work?

The book contains two distinct sets of papers, along with full answers and a Progress Chart:

- Focus tests, accompanied by advice and directions, which are focused on particular (and age-appropriate) Non-verbal Reasoning question types encountered in the 11+ and other exams, but devised at a higher level than the standard Assessment papers. Each Focus test is designed to help raise a child's skills in the question type, as well as offer plenty of practice for the necessary techniques.

- Mixed papers, which are full-length tests containing a full range of Non-verbal Reasoning question types. These are designed to provide rigorous practice for children working at a level higher than that required to pass at the 11+ and other Non-verbal Reasoning tests.

- Full answers are provided for both types of test in the middle of the book.

- At the back of the book, there is a Progress Chart which allows you to track your child's progress. In the Mixed papers we have aligned question types with numbers, so you can identify where your child is performing well or struggling.

How much time should the tests take?

The tests are for practice and to reinforce learning, and you may wish to test exam techniques and working to a set time limit. We would recommend your child spends 35 minutes to answer the 64 questions in each Mixed paper. You can reduce the suggested time by five minutes to practise working at speed.

Using the Progress Chart

The Progress Chart can be used to track Focus test and Mixed paper results over time to monitor how well your child is doing and identify any repeated problems in tackling the different question types.

Focus test 1 Similarities

Which of the shapes belongs to the group on the left? Circle the letter.

Example

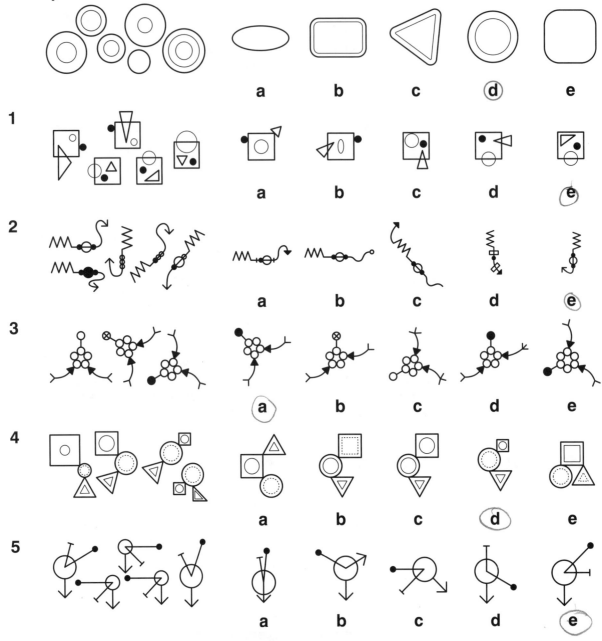

If more than one option looks possible, select
the one that gives the best or closest match.

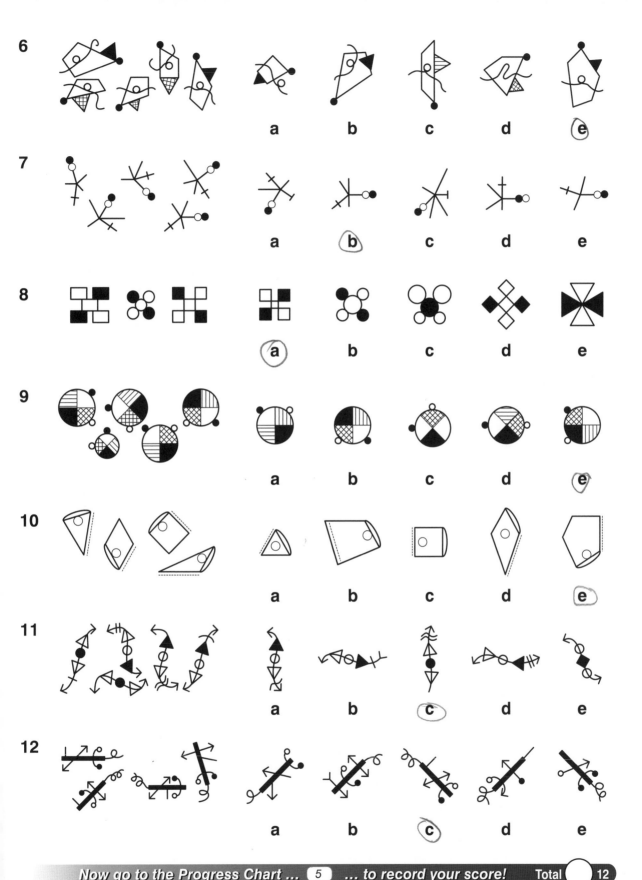

Focus test 2 — Grids

Which shape or pattern completes the pattern on the left? Circle the letter.

Example

a   b   (c)   d   e

> When looking at grids remember the patterns or sequences may go across the rows, down the columns or both ...

1

a   (b)   c   d   e

2

a   (b)   c   d   e

> ... or the whole grid may have a pattern.

3

a   b   c   d   e

4

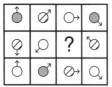

a   b   c   d   e

> A sequence may continue from one row to the next.

5

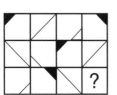

a   b   c   d   e

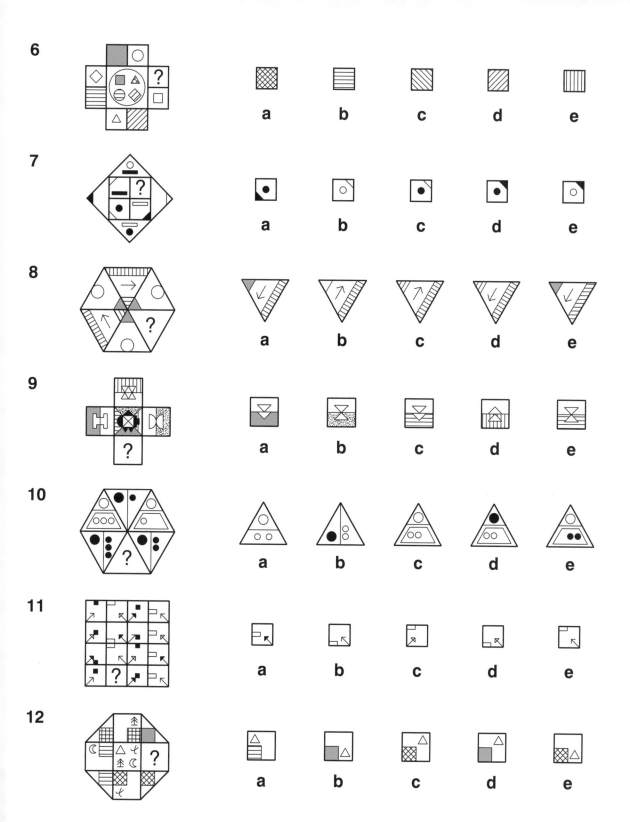

Focus test 3 Analogies

Which shape or pattern completes the second pair in the same way as the first pair? Circle the letter.

Example

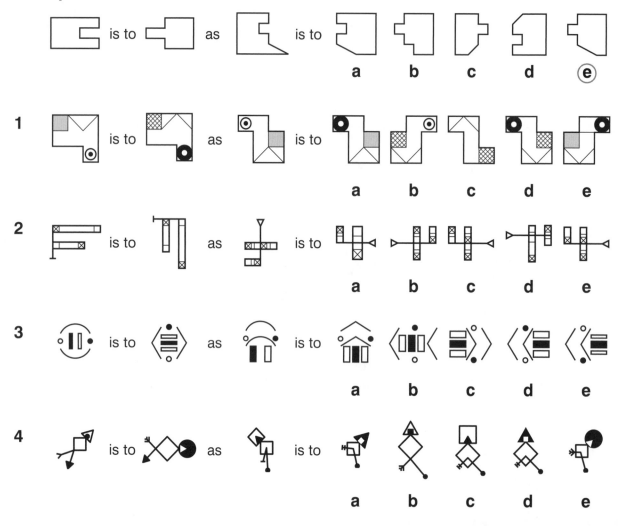

If you think that you can give a reason for more than one answer being correct, look carefully again at the first given pair and then choose the closest match.

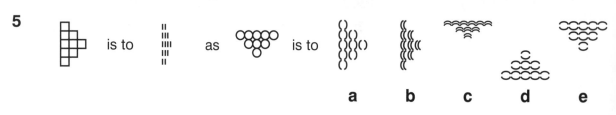

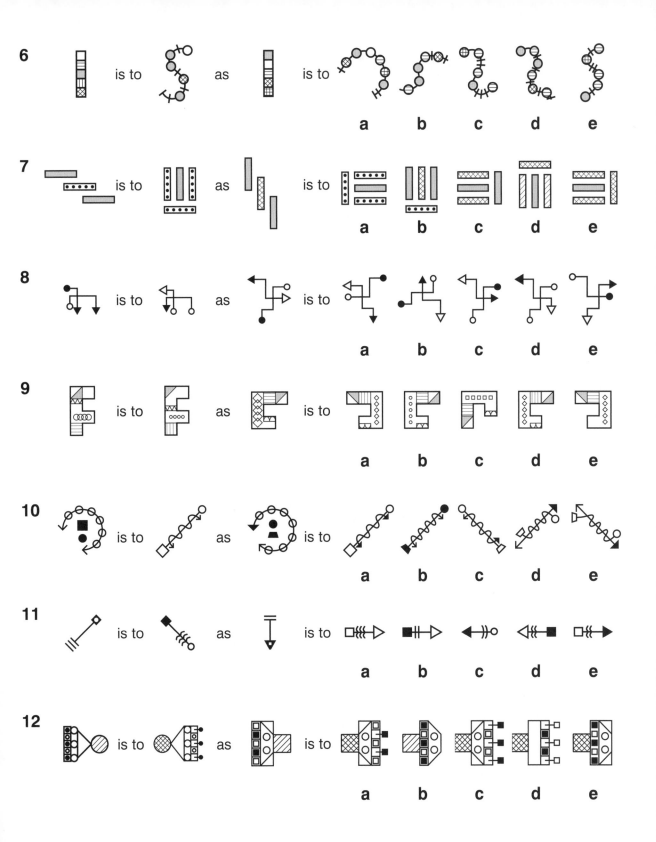

Reflections

Which shape or pattern is a reflection of the shape on the left? Circle the letter.

Example

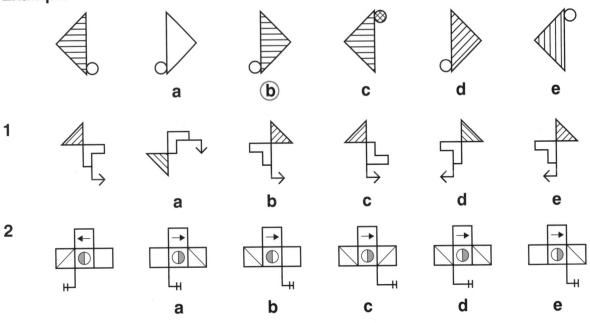

1

2

> The line of reflection for these patterns may be above,
> below or at either side of the shape or pattern.

3

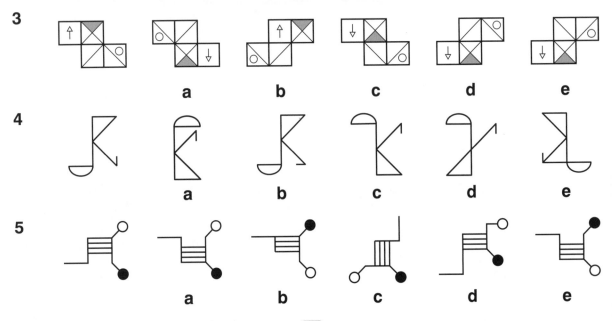

4

5

The line of reflection may also be on the diagonal.

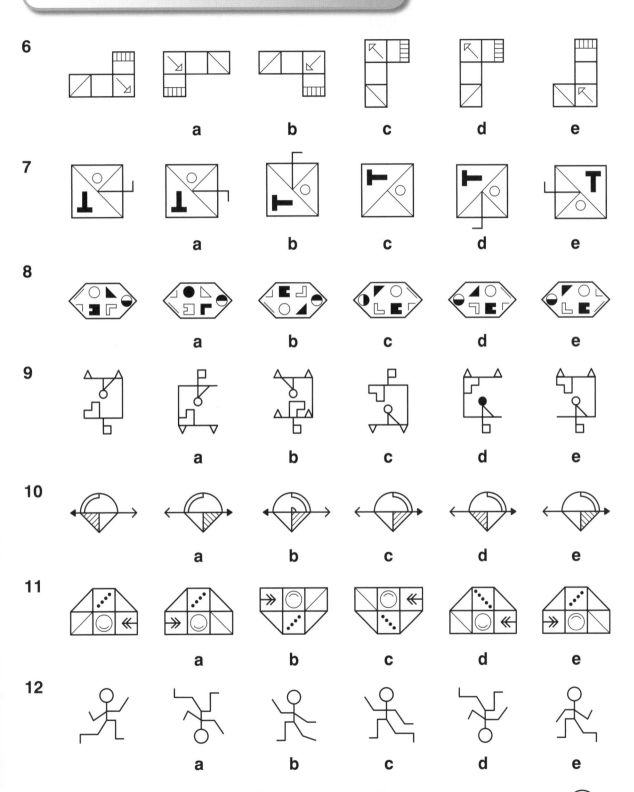

6   a   b   c   d   e

7   a   b   c   d   e

8   a   b   c   d   e

9   a   b   c   d   e

10   a   b   c   d   e

11   a   b   c   d   e

12   a   b   c   d   e

Which shape or pattern continues or completes the given sequence?
Circle the letter.

Example

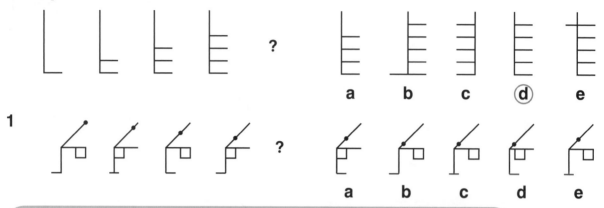

a   b   c   (d)   e

1

a   b   c   d   e

> A sequence may be made up of two different sequences alternating.

2

a   b   c   d   e

3

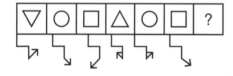 

a   b   c   d   e

> To fill a gap in a sequence work forward and then check by also looking back.

4

a   b   c   d   e

5

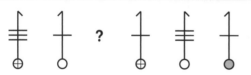

a   b   c   d   e

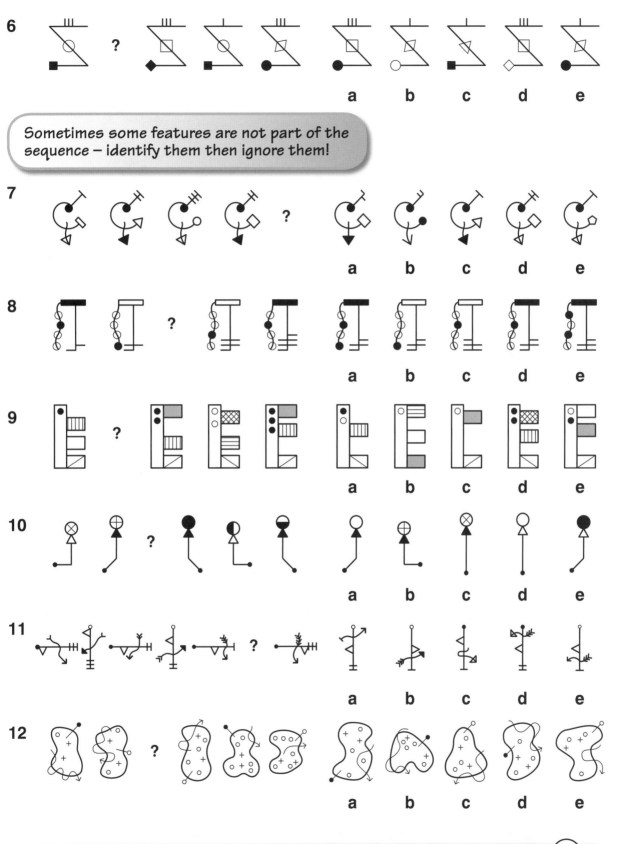

6   ?   **a**   **b**   **c**   **d**   **e**

> Sometimes some features are not part of the
> sequence – identify them then ignore them!

7   ?   **a**   **b**   **c**   **d**   **e**

8   ?   **a**   **b**   **c**   **d**   **e**

9   ?   **a**   **b**   **c**   **d**   **e**

10   ?   **a**   **b**   **c**   **d**   **e**

11   ?   **a**   **b**   **c**   **d**   **e**

12   ?   **a**   **b**   **c**   **d**   **e**

Focus test 6 Cubes

Which cube could not be made from the given net? Circle the letter.

Example

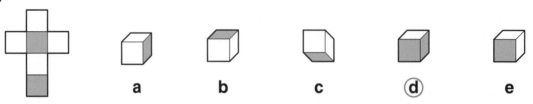

For each type of net, identify the faces that could not end up adjacent (next to each other) in the cube. Always look carefully at the direction of any arrows or shading lines.

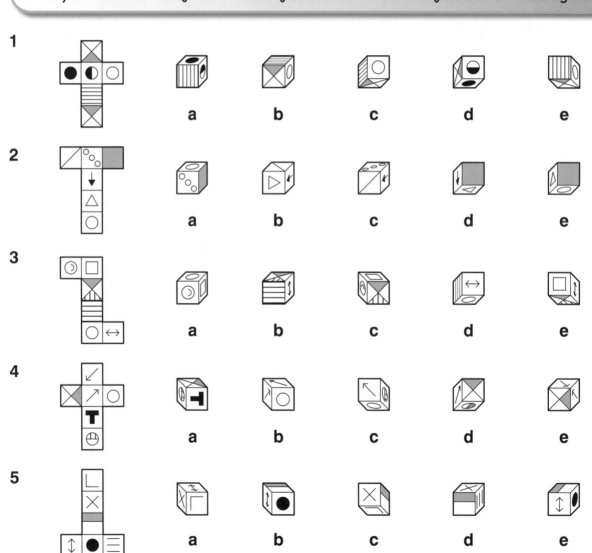

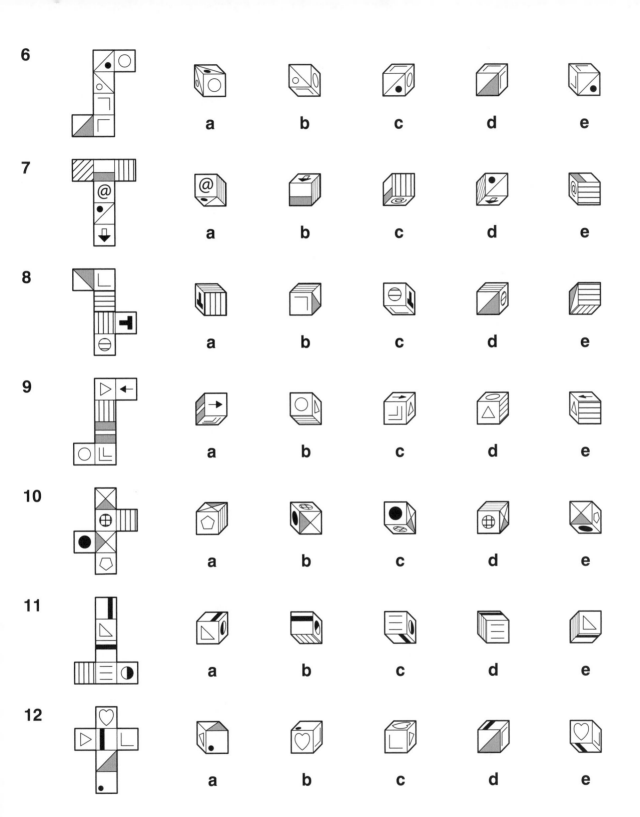

Focus test 7 Codes

Using the given patterns and codes, work out the code that matches the last pattern. Circle the letter.

Example

						AZ	CX	CZ	BY	CY
AX	AY	BZ	CY	BX	?	a	b	ⓒ	d	e

At this level you may have to work out codes by deduction, they are not always in the examples given.

1

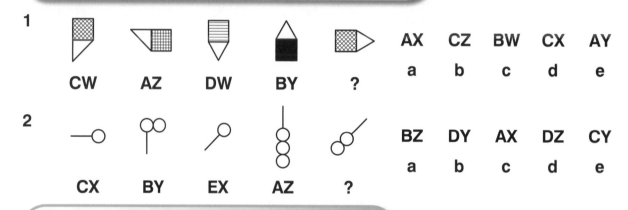

					AX	CZ	BW	CX	AY
CW	AZ	DW	BY	?	a	b	c	d	e

2

					BZ	DY	AX	DZ	CY
CX	BY	EX	AZ	?	a	b	c	d	e

Extra features may be added that are not linked to the code – don't be distracted by them!

3

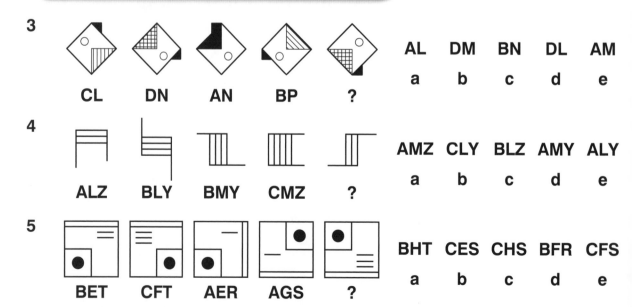

						AL	DM	BN	DL	AM
CL	DN	AN	BP	?		a	b	c	d	e

4

					AMZ	CLY	BLZ	AMY	ALY
ALZ	BLY	BMY	CMZ	?	a	b	c	d	e

5

					BHT	CES	CHS	BFR	CFS
BET	CFT	AER	AGS	?	a	b	c	d	e

Sometimes part of the code appears to be able to link with one or two different features – the answer options may help you to identify the correct one.

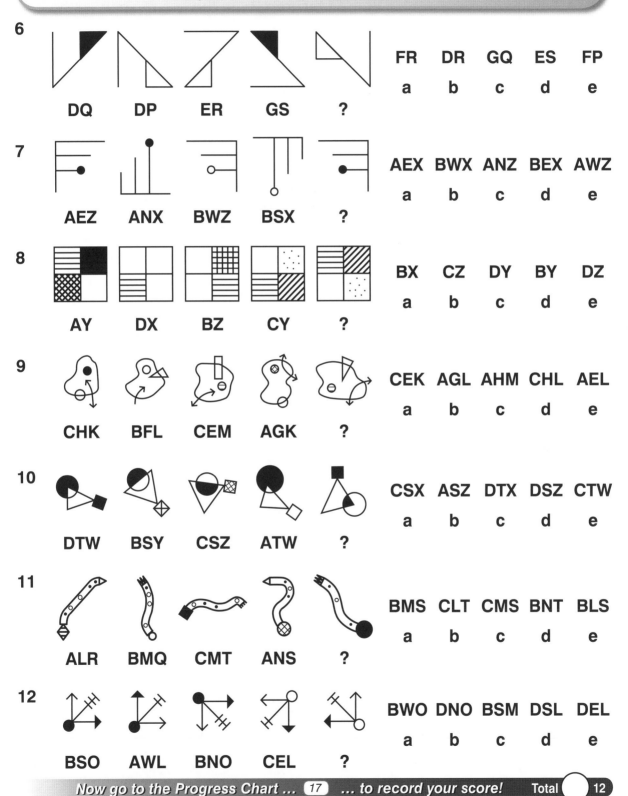

6

DQ DP ER GS ?

FR DR GQ ES FP
a   b   c   d   e

7

AEZ ANX BWZ BSX ?

AEX BWX ANZ BEX AWZ
a   b   c   d   e

8

AY DX BZ CY ?

BX CZ DY BY DZ
a   b   c   d   e

9

CHK BFL CEM AGK ?

CEK AGL AHM CHL AEL
a   b   c   d   e

10

DTW BSY CSZ ATW ?

CSX ASZ DTX DSZ CTW
a   b   c   d   e

11

ALR BMQ CMT ANS ?

BMS CLT CMS BNT BLS
a   b   c   d   e

12

BSO AWL BNO CEL ?

BWO DNO BSM DSL DEL
a   b   c   d   e

Which pattern on the right is formed by combining the two shapes on the left? Circle the letter.

Example

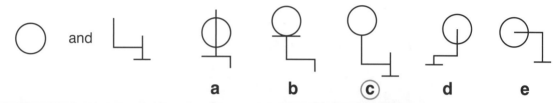

a b c d e

> In these questions it is important to remember that patterns may be rotated, but not turned over – like jigsaw puzzle pieces.

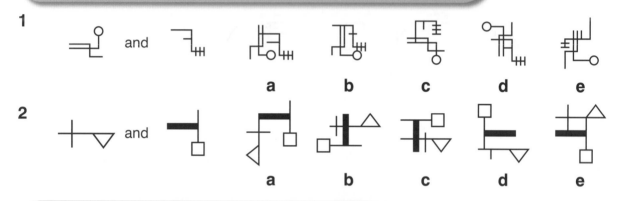

1 and a b c d e

2 and a b c d e

> Separate 2-D shapes may share an edge in the combined shape, but line features will not overlap.

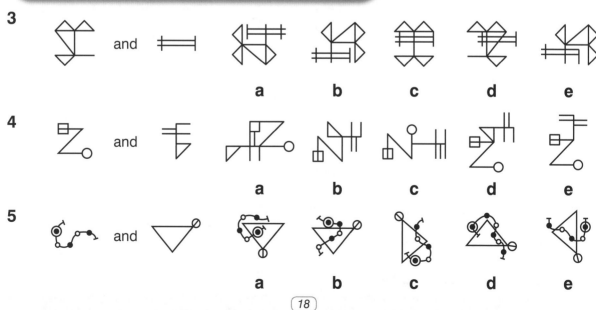

3 and a b c d e

4 and a b c d e

5 and a b c d e

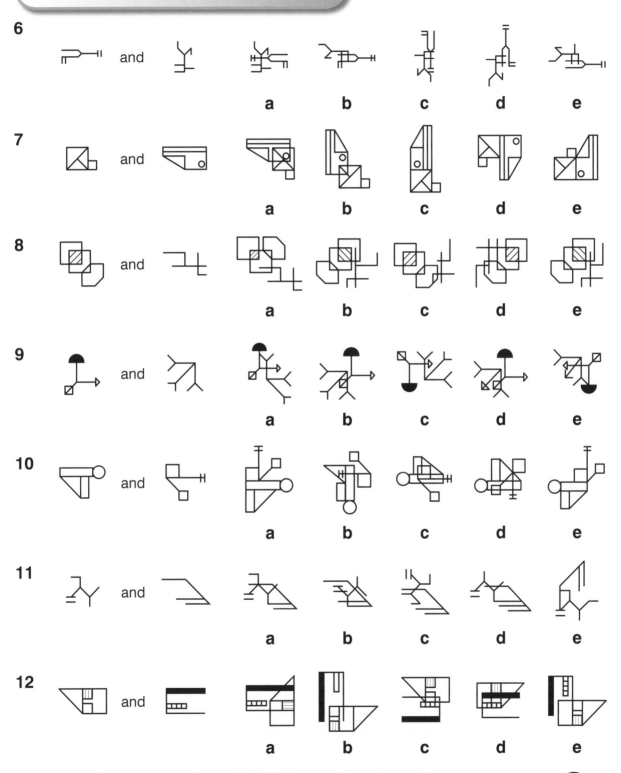

Mixed paper 1

Which of the shapes belongs to the group on the left? Circle the letter.

Example

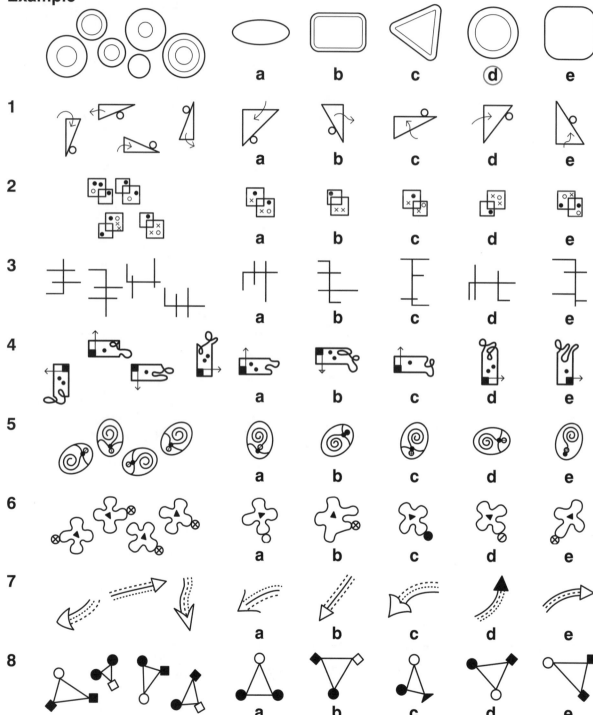

Mixed paper 1

Which shape or pattern completes the pattern on the left? Circle the letter.

Example

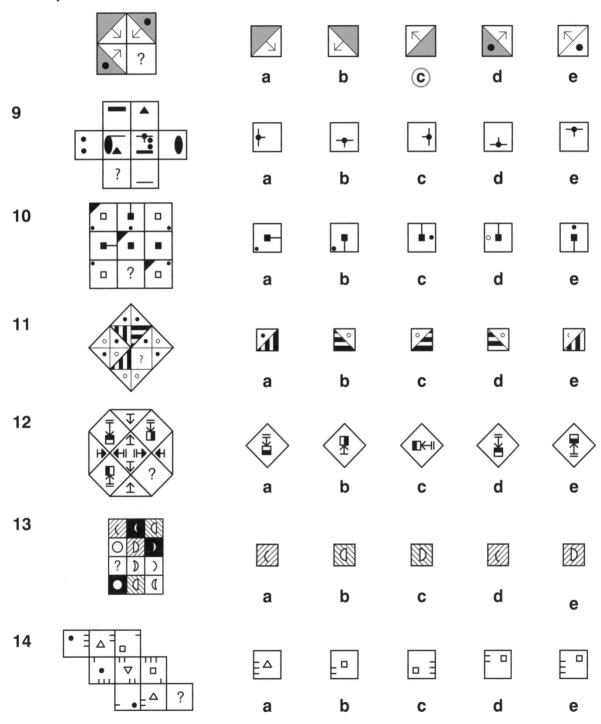

15

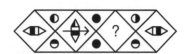

a   b   c   d   e

16

a   b   c   d   e

Mixed paper 1

Which shape or pattern completes the second pair in the same way as the first pair? Circle the letter.

Example

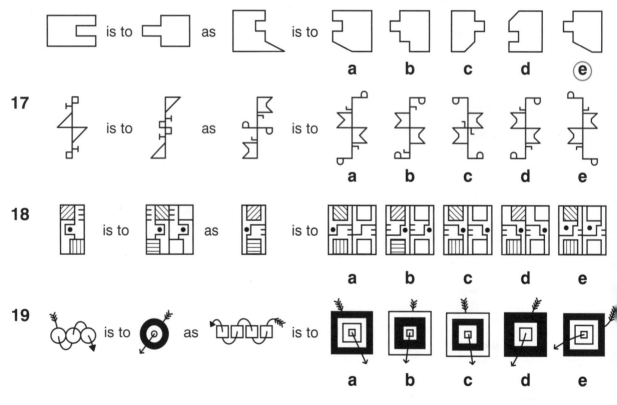

21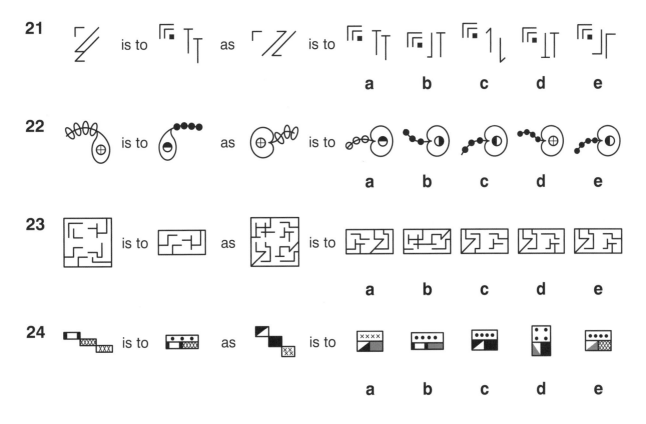

22

23

24

Mixed paper 1

Which shape or pattern is a reflection of the shape on the left? Circle the letter.

Example

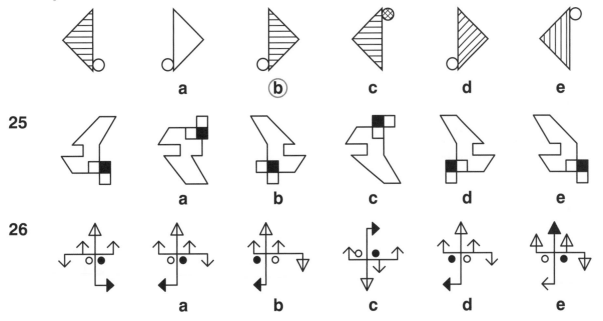

25

a   b   c   d   e

26

a   b   c   d   e

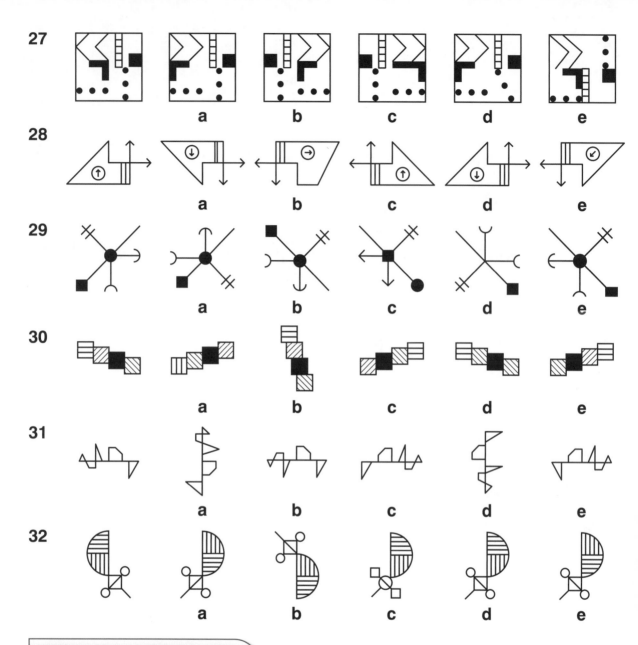

27 a b c d e

28 a b c d e

29 a b c d e

30 a b c d e

31 a b c d e

32 a b c d e

Mixed paper 1

Which shape or pattern continues or completes the given sequence?
Circle the letter.

Example

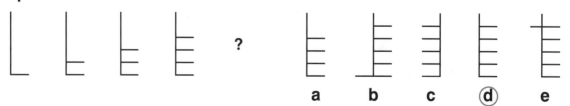

a   b   c   (d)   e

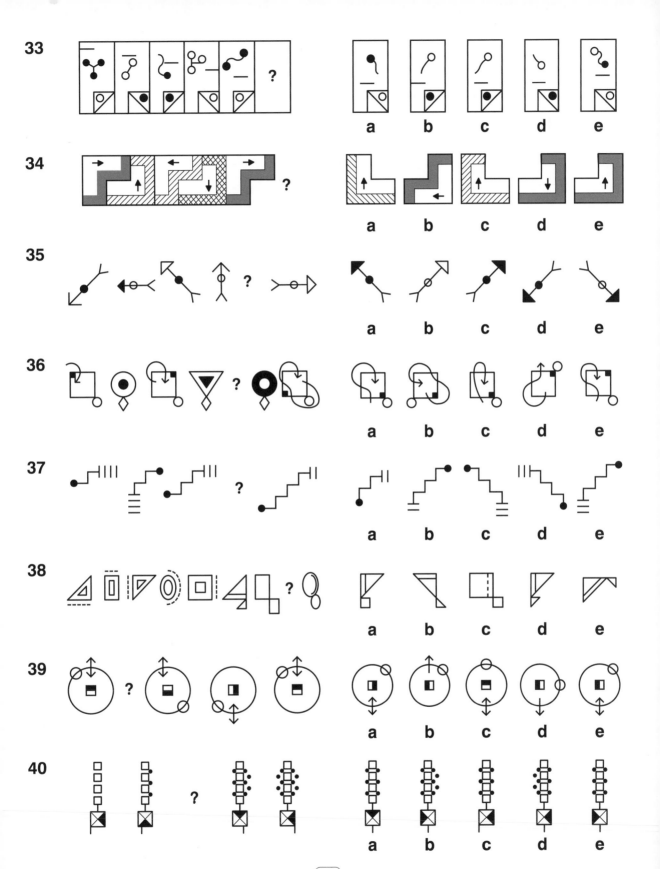

Mixed paper 1

Which cube could not be made from the given net? Circle the letter.

Example

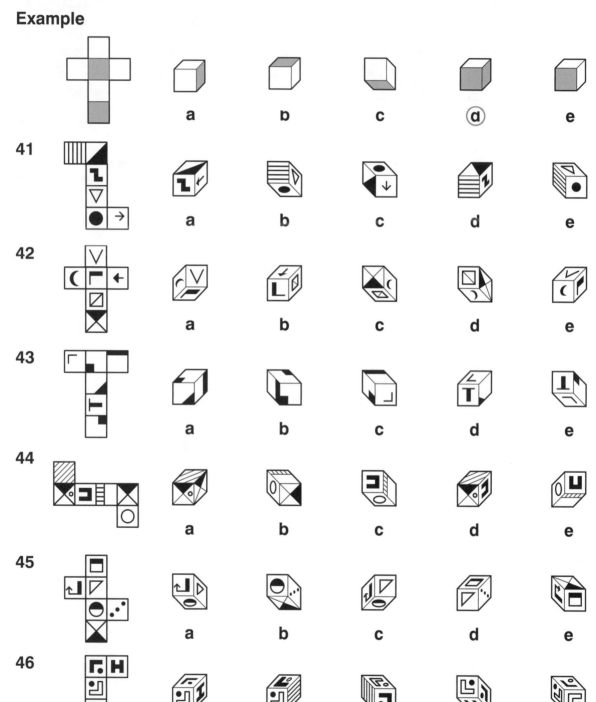

41

42

43

44

45

46

a   b   c   d   e

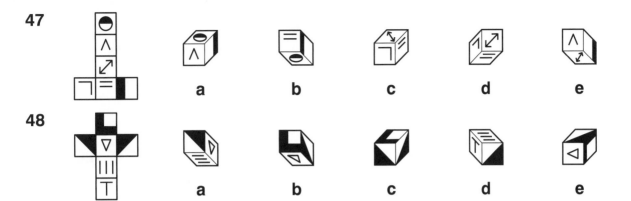

47 a b c d e

48 a b c d e

Mixed paper 1

Using the given patterns and codes, work out the code that matches the last pattern. Circle the letter.

Example

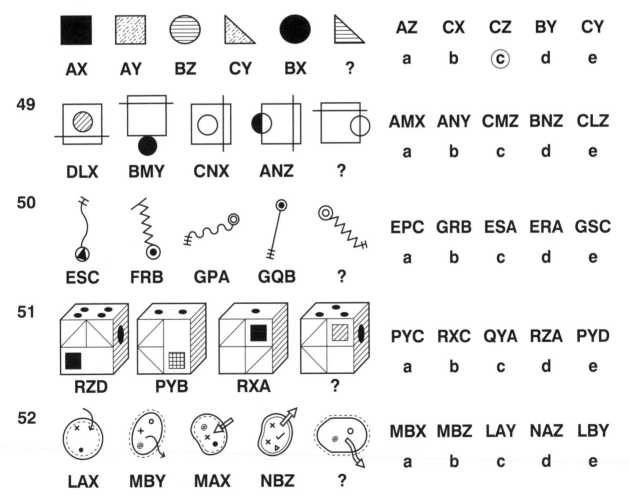

AZ	CX	CZ	BY	CY
a	b	ⓒ	d	e

49

AMX	ANY	CMZ	BNZ	CLZ
a	b	c	d	e

50

EPC	GRB	ESA	ERA	GSC
a	b	c	d	e

51

PYC	RXC	QYA	RZA	PYD
a	b	c	d	e

52

MBX	MBZ	LAY	NAZ	LBY
a	b	c	d	e

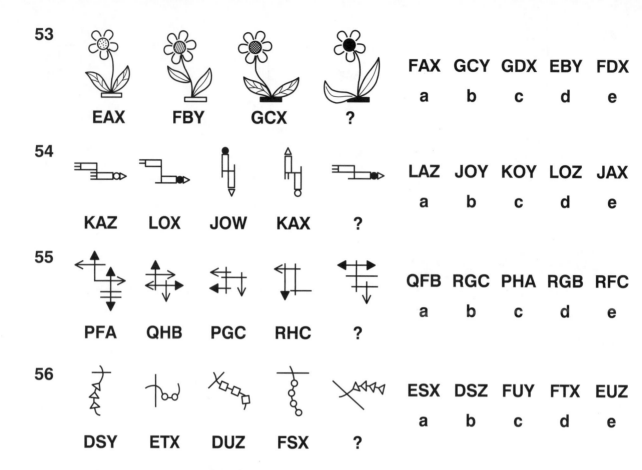

53

EAX   FBY   GCX   ?

FAX	GCY	GDX	EBY	FDX
a	b	c	d	e

54

KAZ   LOX   JOW   KAX   ?

LAZ	JOY	KOY	LOZ	JAX
a	b	c	d	e

55

PFA   QHB   PGC   RHC   ?

QFB	RGC	PHA	RGB	RFC
a	b	c	d	e

56

DSY   ETX   DUZ   FSX   ?

ESX	DSZ	FUY	FTX	EUZ
a	b	c	d	e

Mixed paper 1

Which pattern on the right is formed by combining the two shapes on the left?
Circle the letter.

Example

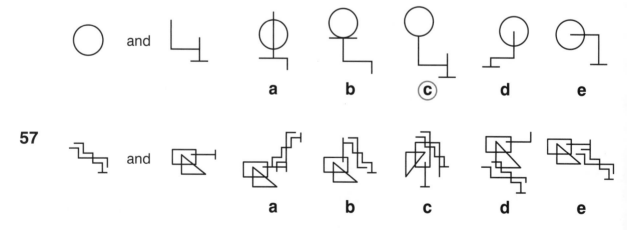

            a   b   ⓒ   d   e

57

            a   b   c   d   e

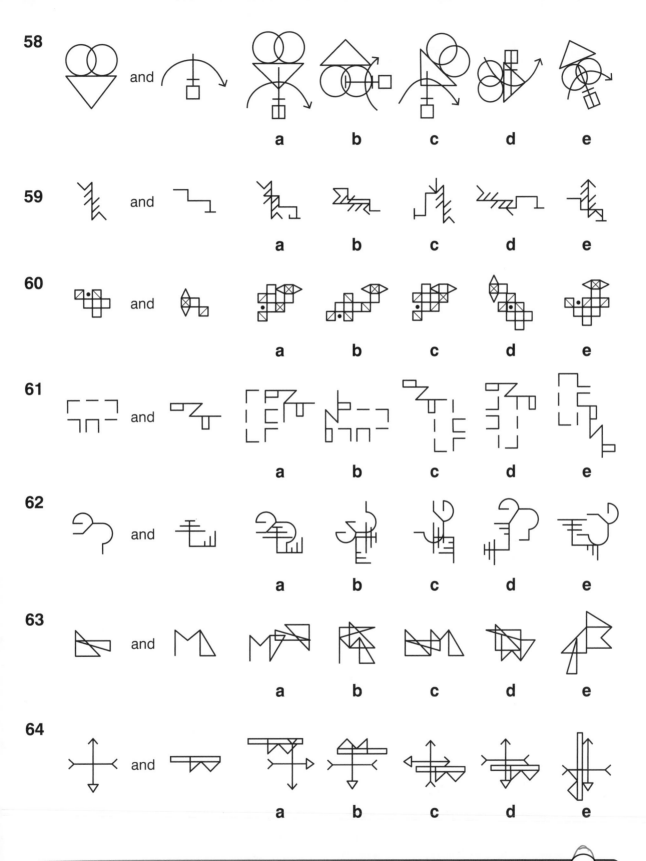

Mixed paper 2

35 mins 1-64

Which of the shapes belongs to the group on the left? Circle the letter.

Example

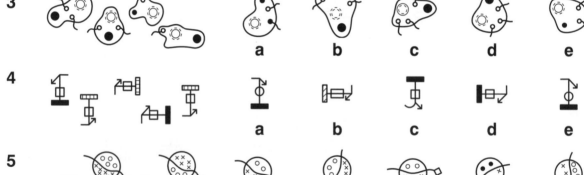

a   b   c   d   e

1   a   b   c   d   e

2   a   b   c   d   e

3   a   b   c   d   e

4   a   b   c   d   e

5   a   b   c   d   e

6   a   b   c   d   e

7   a   b   c   d   e

8   a   b   c   d   e

Mixed paper 2

Which shape or pattern completes the pattern on the left? Circle the letter.

Example

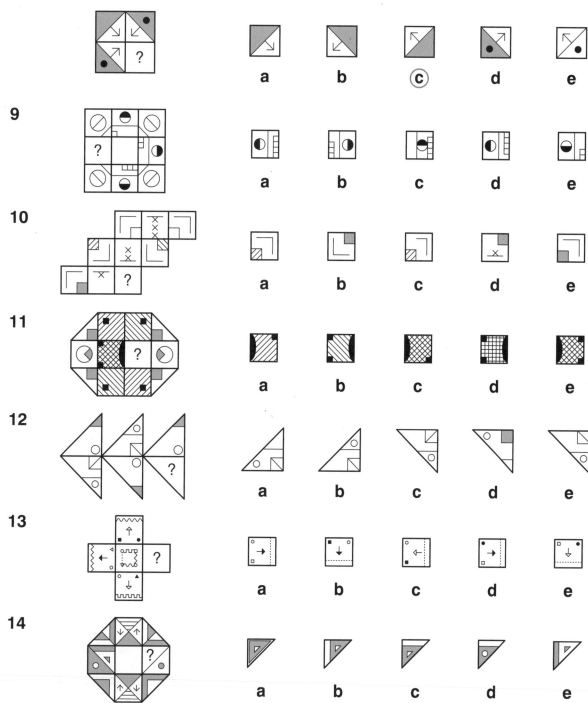

15

                                   a   **b**   **c**   **d**   **e**

16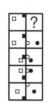

                                   a   **b**   **c**   **d**   **e**

Mixed paper 2

Which shape or pattern completes the second pair in the same way as the first pair? Circle the letter.

Example

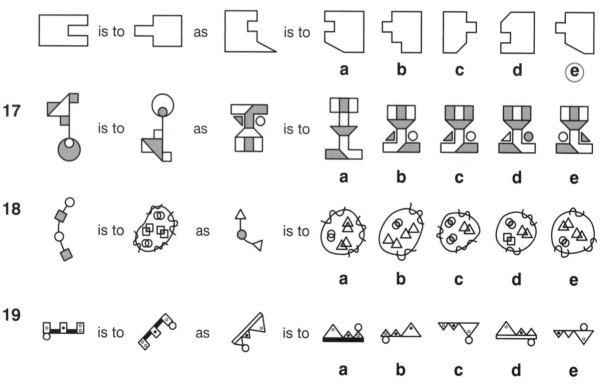

21

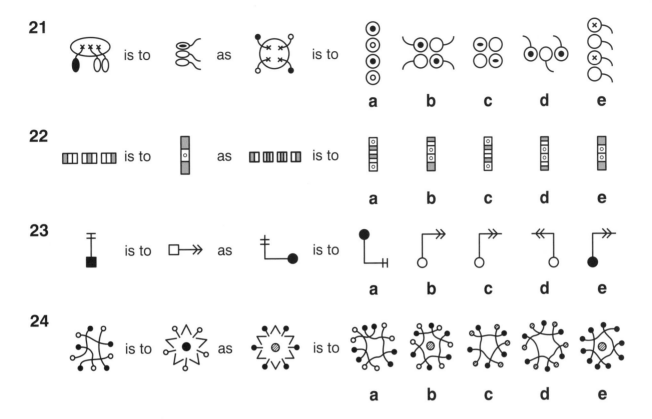

22

a   b   c   d   e

23

a   b   c   d   e

24

a   b   c   d   e

Mixed paper 2

Which shape or pattern is a reflection of the shape on the left? Circle the letter.

Example

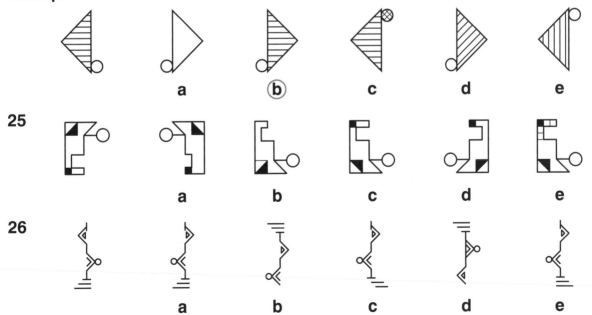

a   (b)   c   d   e

25

a   b   c   d   e

26

a   b   c   d   e

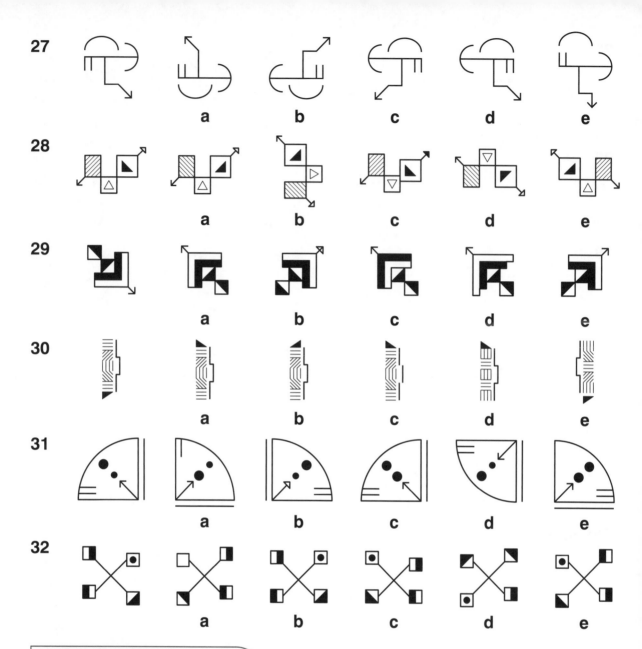

Mixed paper 2

Which shape or pattern continues or completes the given sequence?
Circle the letter.

Example

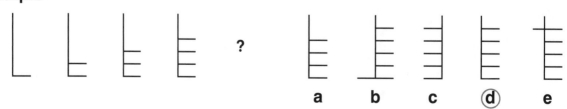

a   b   c   d   e

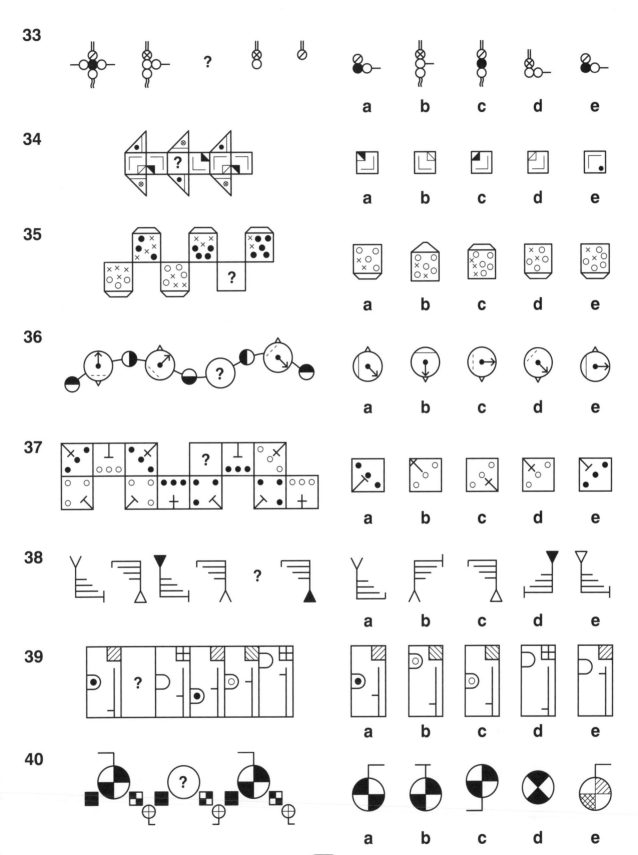

33

a b c d e

34

a b c d e

35

a b c d e

36

a b c d e

37

a b c d e

38

a b c d e

39

a b c d e

40

a b c d e

Mixed paper 2

Which cube could not be made from the given net? Circle the letter.

Example

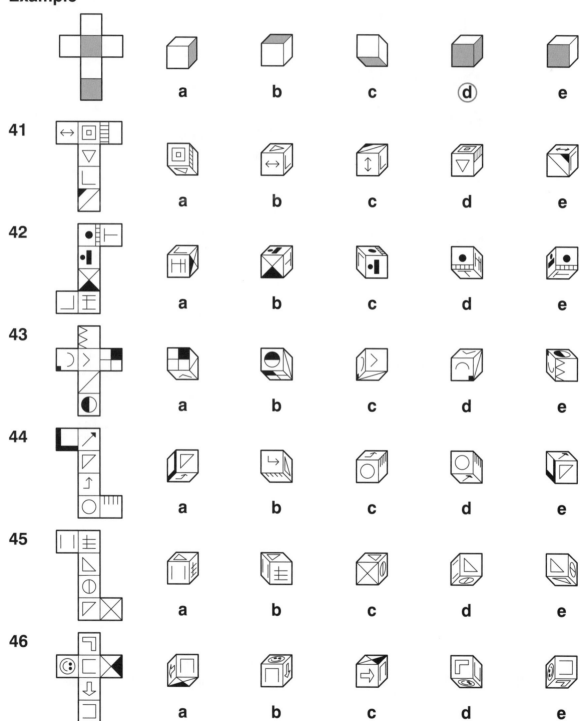

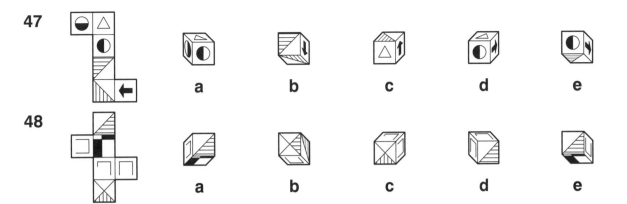

47   a   b   c   d   e

48   a   b   c   d   e

Mixed paper 2

Using the given patterns and codes, work out the code that matches the last pattern. Circle the letter.

Example

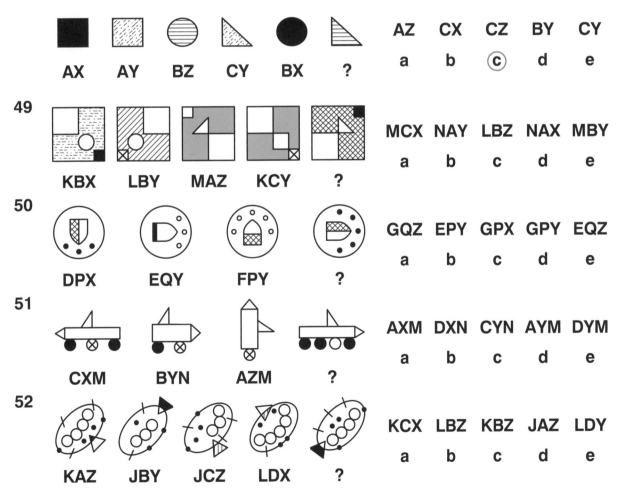

	AZ	CX	CZ	BY	CY
	a	b	©c	d	e

49

	MCX	NAY	LBZ	NAX	MBY
	a	b	c	d	e

50

	GQZ	EPY	GPX	GPY	EQZ
	a	b	c	d	e

51

	AXM	DXN	CYN	AYM	DYM
	a	b	c	d	e

52

	KCX	LBZ	KBZ	JAZ	LDY
	a	b	c	d	e

53

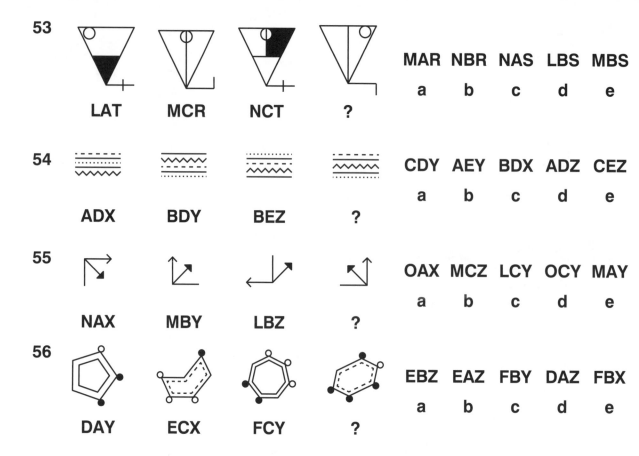

53

LAT	MCR	NCT	?

MAR NBR NAS LBS MBS
a   b   c   d   e

54

ADX	BDY	BEZ	?

CDY AEY BDX ADZ CEZ
a   b   c   d   e

55

NAX	MBY	LBZ	?

OAX MCZ LCY OCY MAY
a   b   c   d   e

56

DAY	ECX	FCY	?

EBZ EAZ FBY DAZ FBX
a   b   c   d   e

Mixed paper 2

Which pattern on the right is made by combining the two shapes on the left? Circle the letter.

Example

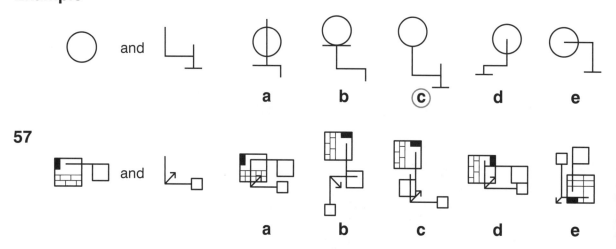

57

a   b   c   d   e

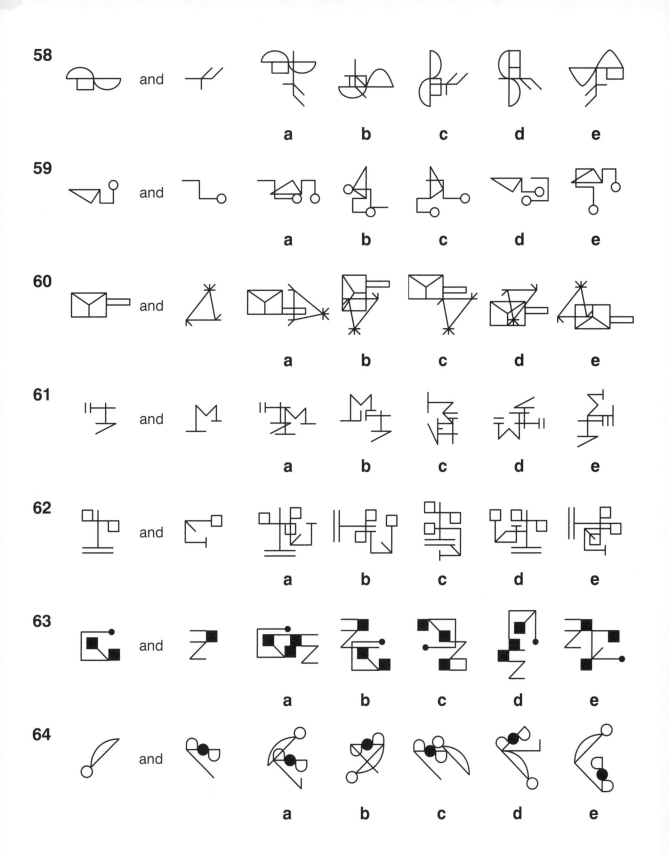

58

59

60

61

62

63

64

a b c d e

Mixed paper 3

35 mins 1-64

Which of the shapes belongs to the group on the left? Circle the letter.

Example

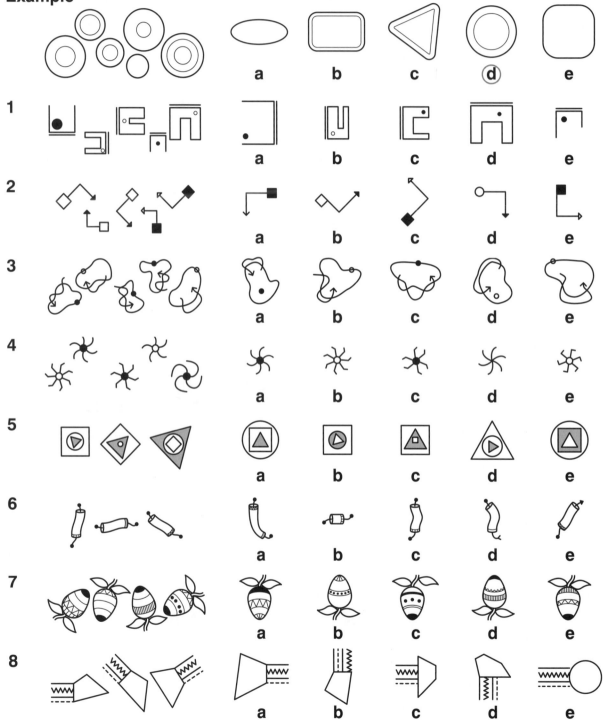

Mixed paper 3

Which shape or pattern completes the pattern on the left? Circle the letter.

Example

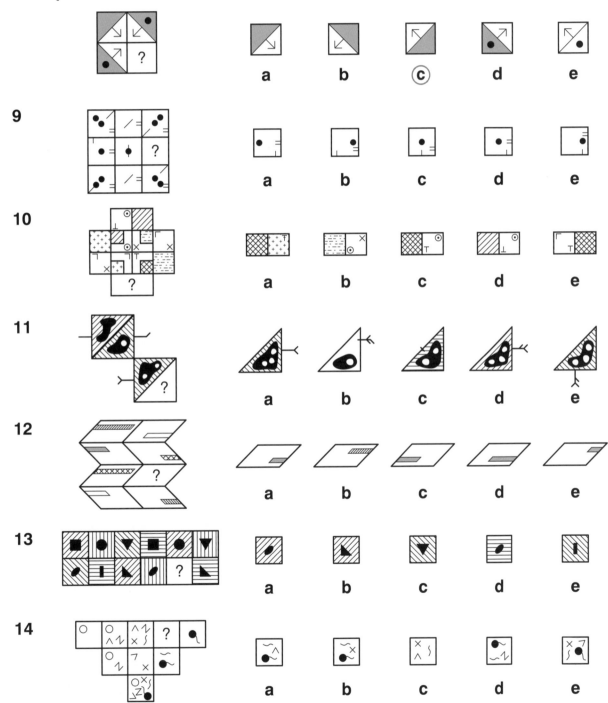

15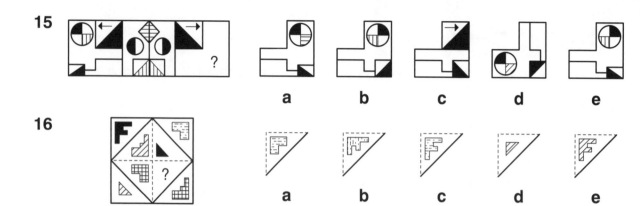

16

Mixed paper 3

Which shape or pattern completes the second pair in the same way as the first pair? Circle the letter.

Example

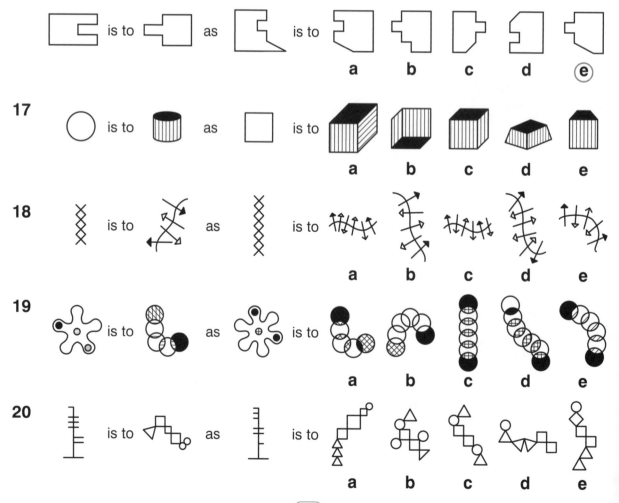

17

18

19

20

21

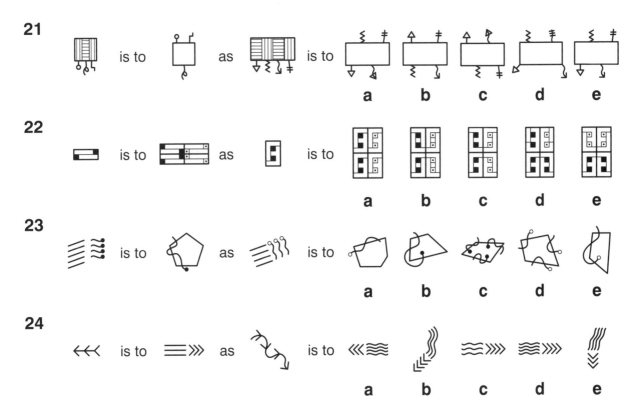

22

23

24

Mixed paper 3

Which shape or pattern is a reflection of the shape on the left? Circle the letter.

Example

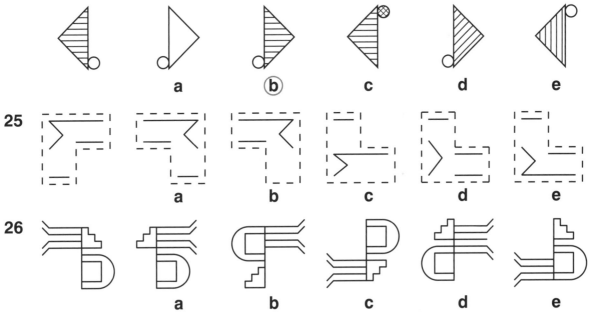

25

26

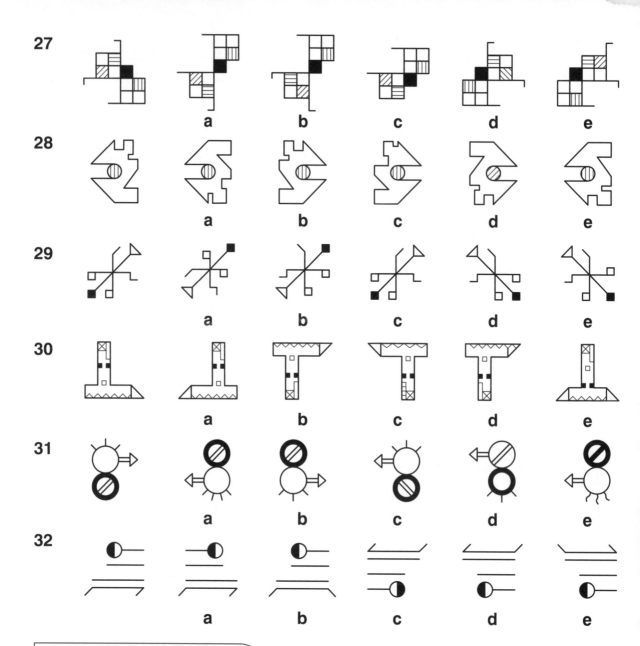

27

28

29

30

31

32

Mixed paper 3

Which shape or pattern continues or completes the given sequence?
Circle the letter.

Example

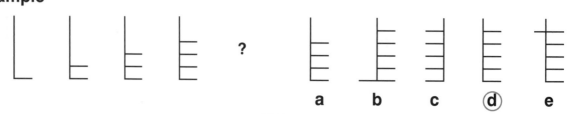

a   b   c   (d)   e

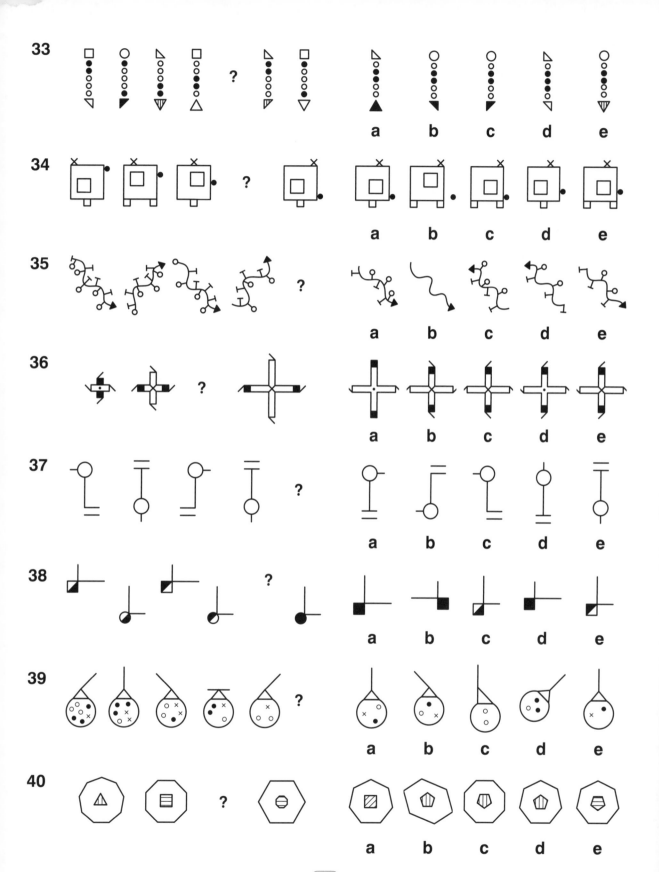

Mixed paper 3

Which cube could not be made from the given net? Circle the letter.

Example

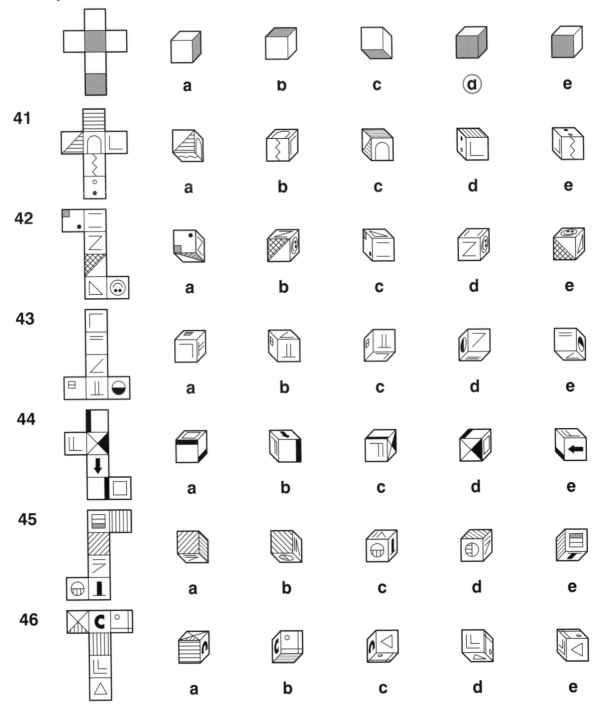

47

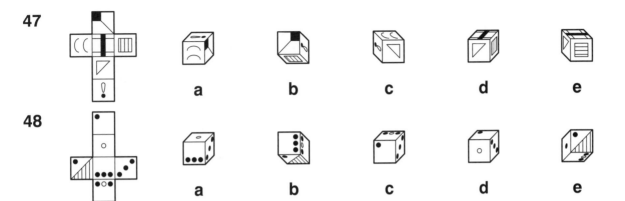

a b c d e

48

a b c d e

Mixed paper 3

Using the given patterns and codes, work out the code that matches the last pattern. Circle the letter.

Example

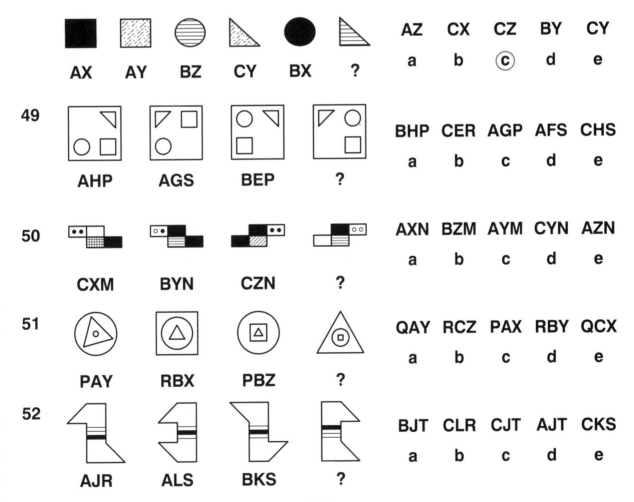

AX AY BZ CY BX ?

AZ CX CZ BY CY
a b ⓒ d e

49

AHP AGS BEP ?

BHP CER AGP AFS CHS
a b c d e

50

CXM BYN CZN ?

AXN BZM AYM CYN AZN
a b c d e

51

PAY RBX PBZ ?

QAY RCZ PAX RBY QCX
a b c d e

52

AJR ALS BKS ?

BJT CLR CJT AJT CKS
a b c d e

53

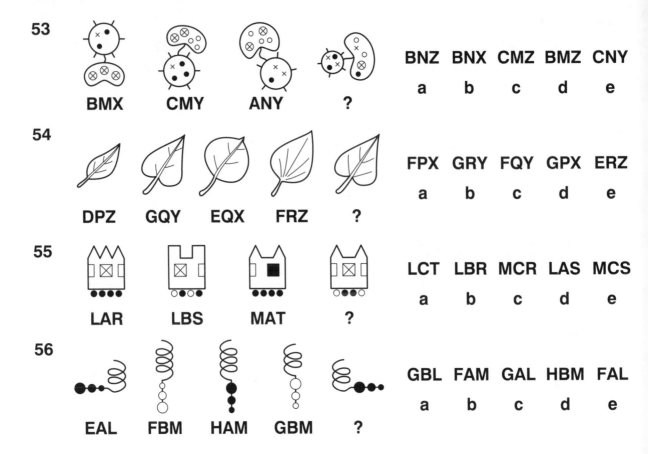

BNZ	BNX	CMZ	BMZ	CNY
a	b	c	d	e

BMX   CMY   ANY   ?

54

FPX	GRY	FQY	GPX	ERZ
a	b	c	d	e

DPZ   GQY   EQX   FRZ   ?

55

LCT	LBR	MCR	LAS	MCS
a	b	c	d	e

LAR   LBS   MAT   ?

56

GBL	FAM	GAL	HBM	FAL
a	b	c	d	e

EAL   FBM   HAM   GBM   ?

Mixed paper 3

Which pattern on the right is made by combining the two shapes on the left?
Circle the letter.

Example

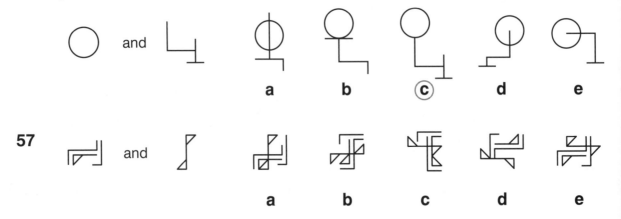

57

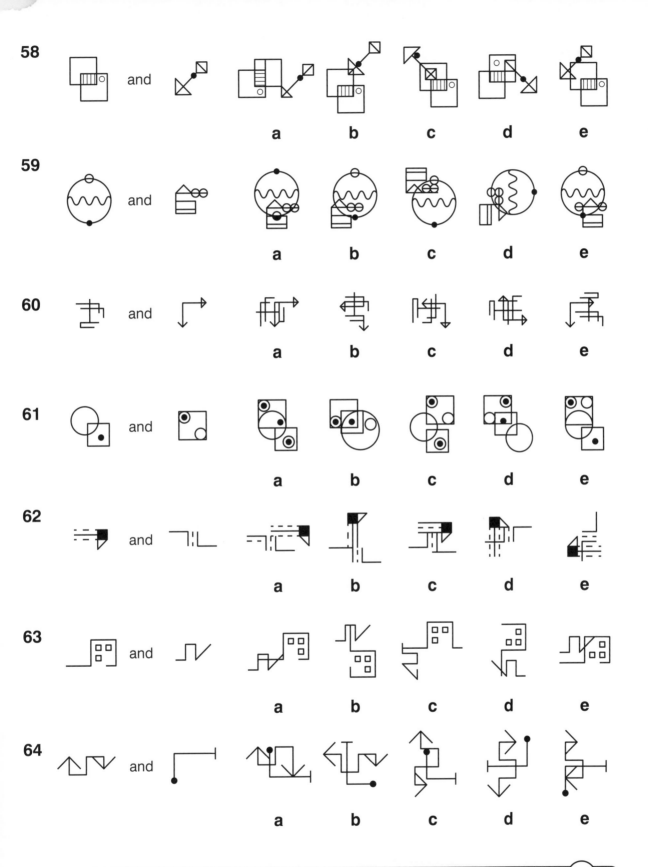

58

59

60

61

62

63

64

Mixed paper 4

35 mins 1-64

Which of the shapes belongs to the group on the left? Circle the letter.

Example

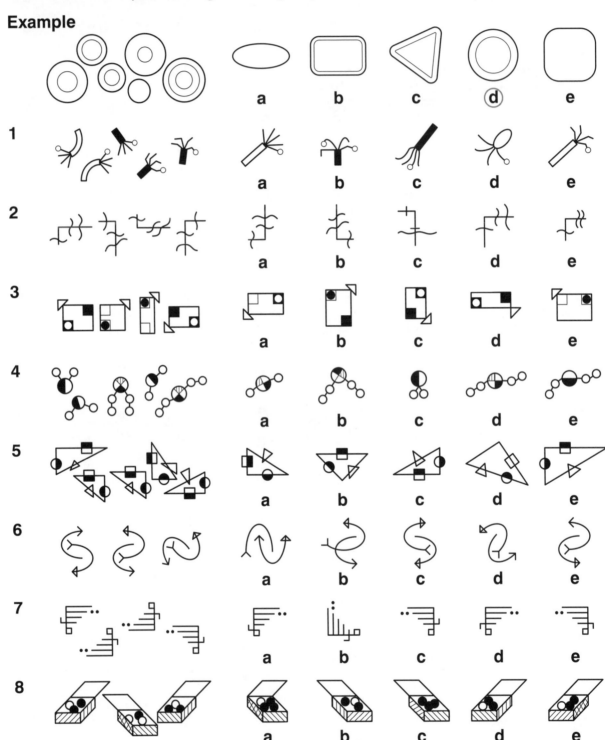

Mixed paper 4

Which shape or pattern completes the pattern on the left? Circle the letter.

Example

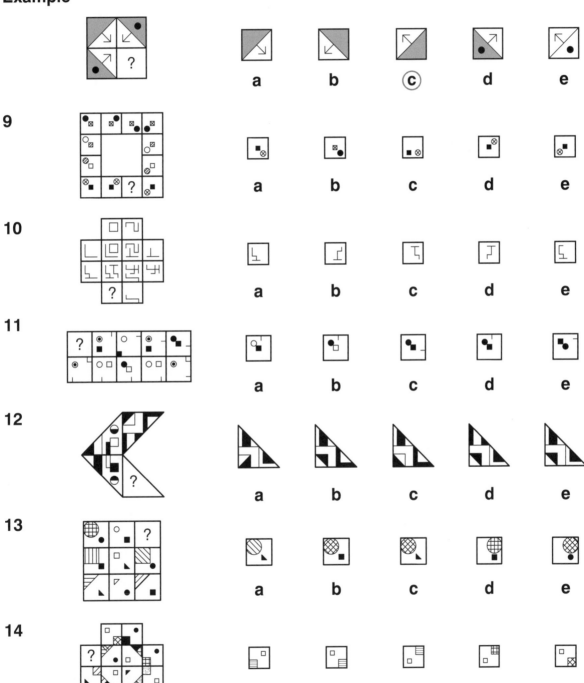

9

10

11

12

13

14

15

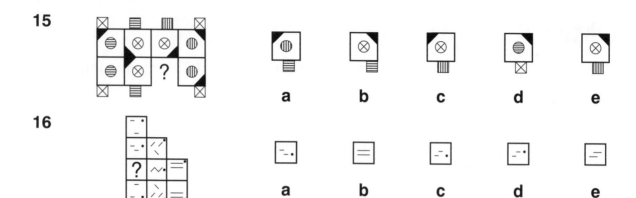

16

Mixed paper 4

Which shape or pattern completes the second pair in the same way as the first pair? Circle the letter.

Example

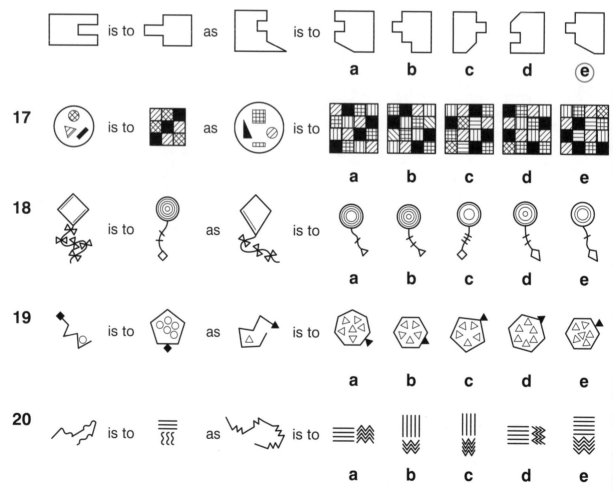

21

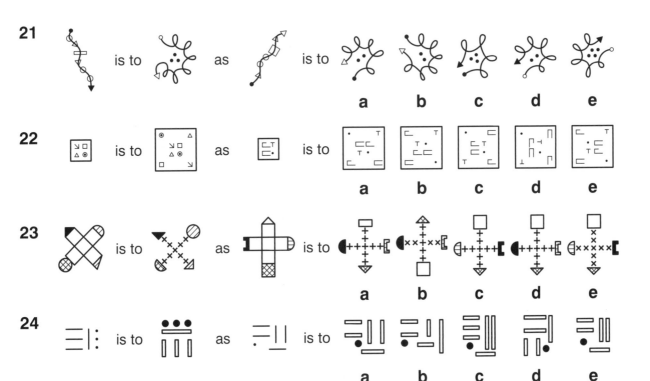

22

23

24

Mixed paper 4

Which shape or pattern is a reflection of the shape on the left? Circle the letter.

Example

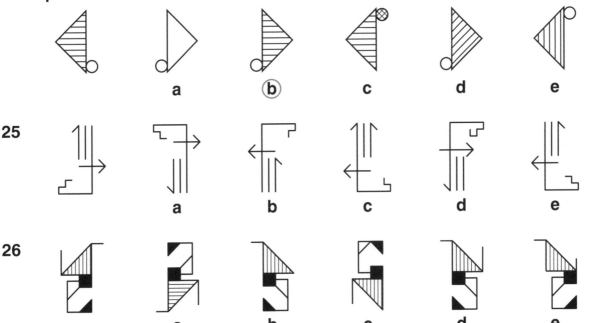

25

26

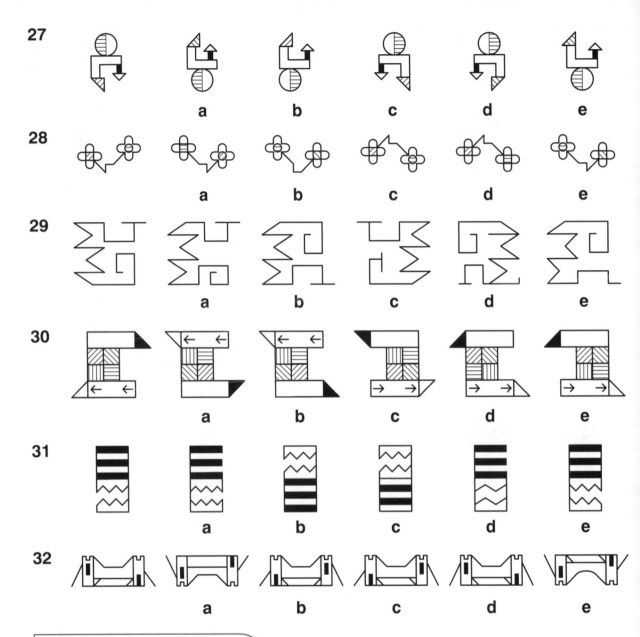

27

      a   **b**   **c**   **d**   **e**

28

      a   **b**   **c**   **d**   **e**

29

      a   **b**   **c**   **d**   **e**

30

      a   **b**   **c**   **d**   **e**

31

      a   **b**   **c**   **d**   **e**

32

      a   **b**   **c**   **d**   **e**

Mixed paper 4

Which shape or pattern continues or completes the given sequence? Circle the letter.

Example

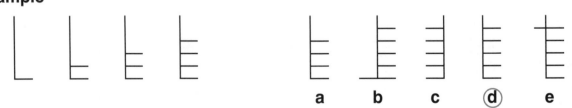

      a   **b**   **c**   **(d)**   **e**

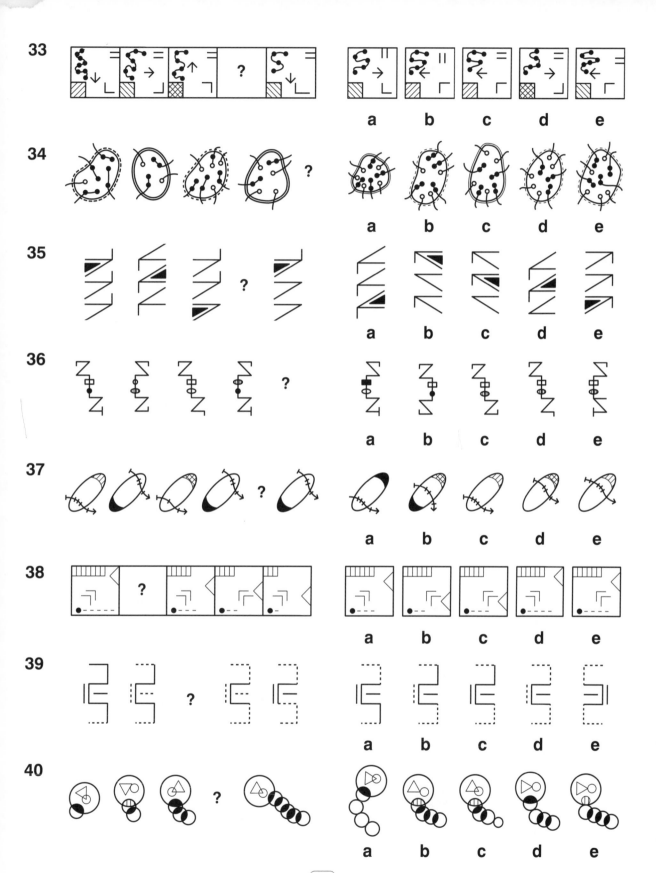

Mixed paper 4

Which cube could not be made from the given net? Circle the letter.

Example

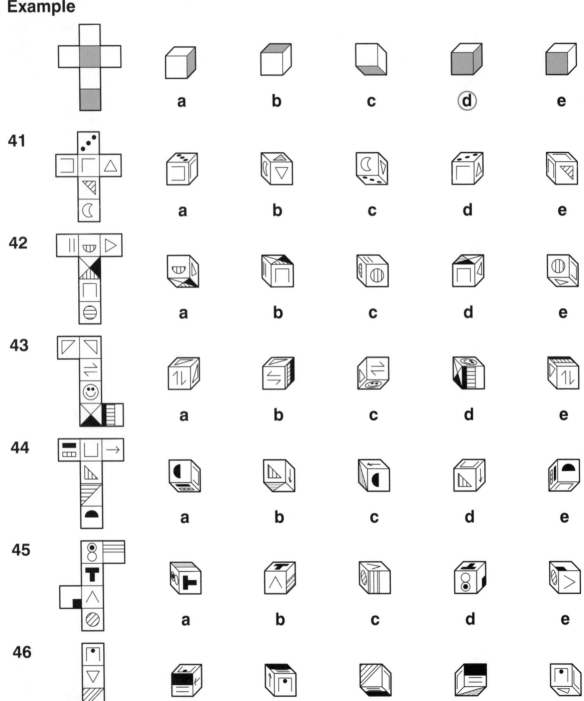

41

42

43

44

45

46

47

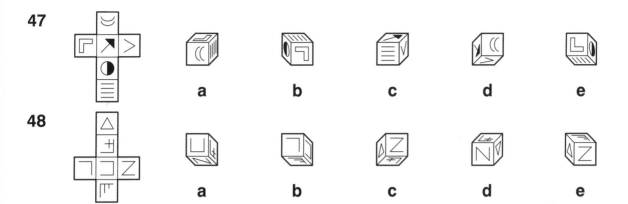

a   b   c   d   e

48

a   b   c   d   e

Mixed paper 4

Using the given patterns and codes, work out the code that matches the last pattern. Circle the letter.

Example

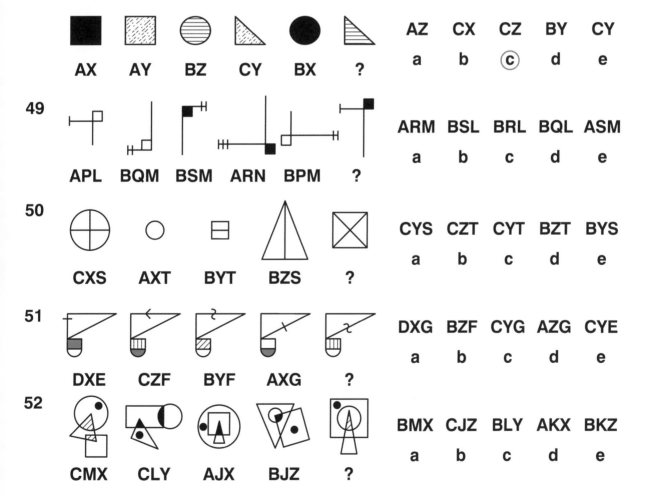

49

APL   BQM   BSM   ARN   BPM   ?

ARM   BSL   BRL   BQL   ASM
a   b   c   d   e

50

CXS   AXT   BYT   BZS   ?

CYS   CZT   CYT   BZT   BYS
a   b   c   d   e

51

DXE   CZF   BYF   AXG   ?

DXG   BZF   CYG   AZG   CYE
a   b   c   d   e

52

CMX   CLY   AJX   BJZ   ?

BMX   CJZ   BLY   AKX   BKZ
a   b   c   d   e

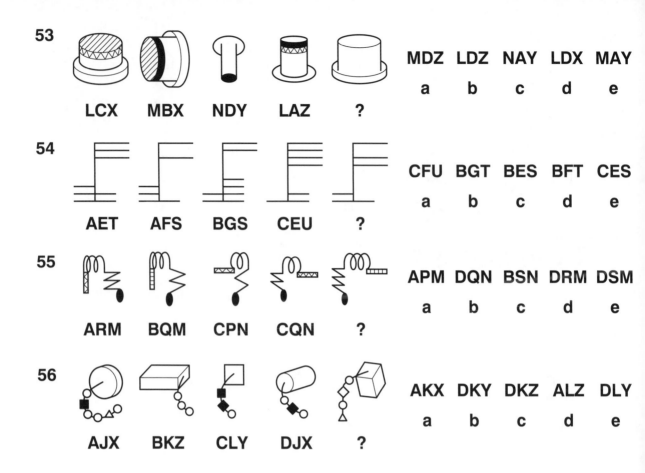

53

LCX   MBX   NDY   LAZ   ?

MDZ   LDZ   NAY   LDX   MAY

a   b   c   d   e

54

AET   AFS   BGS   CEU   ?

CFU   BGT   BES   BFT   CES

a   b   c   d   e

55

ARM   BQM   CPN   CQN   ?

APM   DQN   BSN   DRM   DSM

a   b   c   d   e

56

AJX   BKZ   CLY   DJX   ?

AKX   DKY   DKZ   ALZ   DLY

a   b   c   d   e

Mixed paper 4

Which pattern on the right is made by combining the two shapes on the left?
Circle the letter.

Example

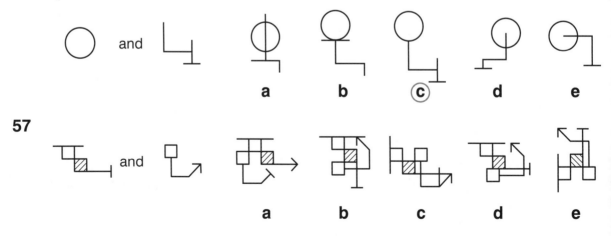

a   b   ⓒ   d   e

57

and

a   b   c   d   e

58

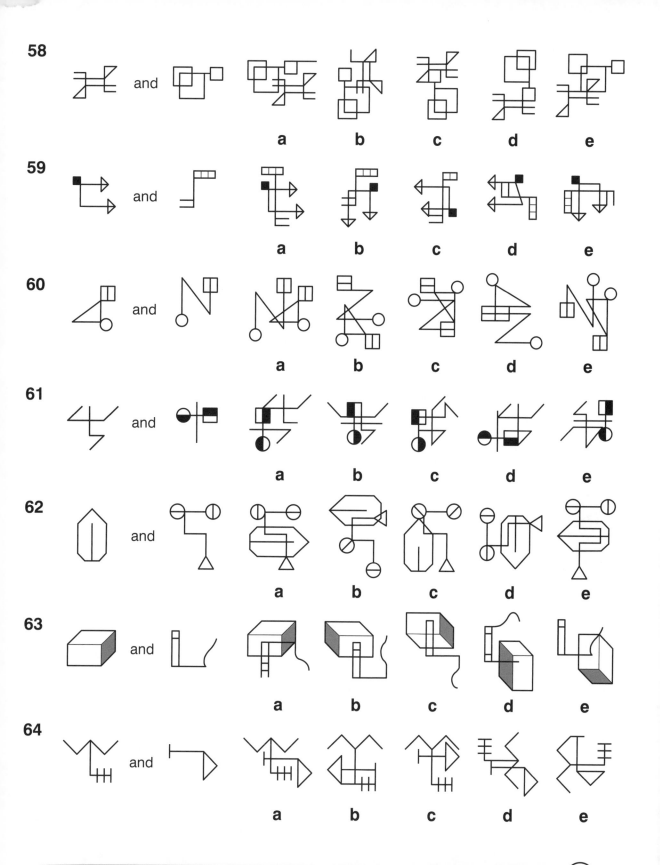

and

a b c d e

59

and

a b c d e

60

and

a b c d e

61

and

a b c d e

62

and

a b c d e

63

and

a b c d e

64

and

a b c d e

Progress Chart

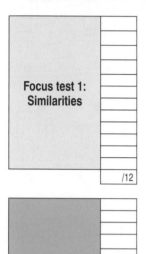

Focus test 1:
Similarities

/12

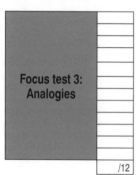

Focus test 2:
Grids

/12

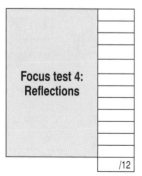

Focus test 3:
Analogies

/12

Focus test 4:
Reflections

/12

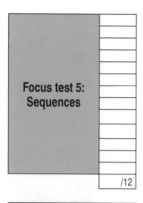

Focus test 5:
Sequences

/12

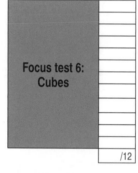

Focus test 6:
Cubes

/12

Focus test 7:
Codes

/12

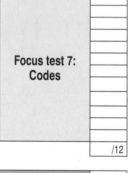

Focus test 8:
Combining
Shapes

/12

	Mixed paper 1	Mixed paper 2	Mixed paper 3	Mixed paper 4	
1					Similarities
2					
3					
4					
5					
6					
7					
8					
9					Grids
10					
11					
12					
13					
14					
15					
16					
17					Analogies
18					
19					
20					
21					
22					
23					
24					
25					Reflections
26					
27					
28					
29					
30					
31					
32					
33					Sequences
34					
35					
36					
37					
38					
39					
40					
41					Cubes
42					
43					
44					
45					
46					
47					
48					
49					Codes
50					
51					
52					
53					
54					
55					
56					
57					Combining shapes
58					
59					
60					
61					
62					
63					
64					
	/64	/64	/64	/64	